Best Editorial Cartoons of the Year

BEST EDITORIAL CARTOONS OF THE YEAR

1978 EDITION

Edited by
CHARLES BROOKS

A FIREBIRD PRESS BOOK

PELICAN PUBLISHING COMPANY
Gretna 1998

Copyright © 1978
By Charles G. Brooks
All rights reserved
ISBN: 88289-192-8
ISBN: 88289-193-6 pb

Manufactured in the United States of America

Published by Pelican Publishing Company, Inc.
1000 Burmaster Street, Gretna, Louisiana 70053

Contents

A Special Tribute to Cy Hungerford 7
Award-Winning Cartoons 8
Carter Administration 13
Bert Lance 25
Andrew Young 34
Korean Scandal 38
Congress 43
The Economy 48
Foreign Relations 56
Human Rights 64
The Middle East 71
Panama Canal 78
Africa 84
Alaskan Pipeline 90
Energy 93
U.S. Defense 105
Terrorism 111
Richard Nixon 114
Bureaucracy 120
Billy Carter 123
The Quebec Question 125
Pollution and Chemicals 128
Education 131
Crime 134
Social Security 139
Medicine 142
Concorde 146
In Memoriam 148
...And Other Issues 151
Past Award Winners 157
Index 159

Cartoons by Hungerford

America's Problem Child —By Hungerford

"Americanism Day" —By Hungerford

A Cartoonist OK for LBJ —By Hungerford

A SPECIAL TRIBUTE TO
Cy Hungerford
Pittsburgh Post-Gazette

74 Years of Editorial Cartooning

Until his retirement in 1977 at the age of 89, Cyrus Cotton Hungerford of the *Pittsburgh Post-Gazette* turned out fresh, lively, imaginative editorial cartoons for 74 years, a standard of longevity that no doubt will remain unmatched in the field of journalism.

For 65 of those distinguished years, Hungerford's work graced the pages of the *Post-Gazette* and its predecessor, the *Pittsburgh Sun*, which he joined in 1912. An institution throughout the state of Pennsylvania, Hungerford projected through his cartoons a rare combination of wit, warmth, insight, compassion, and an uplifting spirit. He enthusiastically caricatured public figures and politicians, and his work spanned the administration of 14 American presidents. Today, offices throughout Pennsylvania and the nation's capitol are decorated with Hungerford originals. More than 2,500 of them are catalogued at Carnegie Library in Pittsburgh.

Hungerford traveled the world in his pursuit of cartoon subjects, paying working visits to Europe, Africa, the Middle East, Mexico, and the West Indies. Along the way he sketched such notable events as the 1937 coronation of King George V, the 1947 marriage of Elizabeth and Prince Philip, and the 1952 coronation of Queen Elizabeth.

Hungerford's career spanned two eras of cartooning. When he began drawing, he would sketch the cartoon on thin chalk paper, trace it in reverse, and finally etch a plate, blowing away the dust throughout the process. Today's method, of course, is somewhat more practical.

One of Hungerford's first chalk paper cartoons, drawn at the tender age of 15, attracted a great deal of attention—and a lawsuit as well. Cy innocently sketched a cartoon depicting a local citizen robbing a bank with one hand and choking a group of helpless widows and orphans with the other. The inexperienced young Hungerford then added the citizen's name in bold, unmistakable strokes. As might have been expected, a libel suit immediately followed. A compassionate district attorney rescued him from his youthful dilemma with a ringing lecture. But as Hungerford often declared later, he had learned his lesson well. In all of his thousands of subsequent editorial cartoons, he never again labeled a banker by name, especially if the banker *was* choking widows and orphans.

After 74 years as an editorial cartoonist, Cy Hungerford can look back upon a distinguished and precedent-setting career. This volume pays tribute to his work.

Award-Winning Cartoons

> For the first time in history, one editorial cartoonist swept the three top awards for editorial cartooning excellence in the United States. Paul Szep of the *Boston Globe* was chosen as having produced the best editorial cartoons of the year by the Pulitzer, the Sigma Delta Chi, and the National Headliners Club award committees.

PAUL SZEP

Editorial Cartoonist
Boston Globe

Born in Hamilton, Ontario, Canada; began working as a sports cartoonist at the age 16; graduated from Ontario College of Art in 1964; worked as a book and fashion illustrator and graphics designer; worked for five years in Canadian steel mills; worked briefly with the Toronto *Financial Post*; joined the *Boston Globe* in 1966 as an editorial cartoonist; won Pulitzer Prize in 1974 and was a previous winner of both the Sigma Delta Chi Award and the National Headliners Club Award; awarded honorary Doctor of Laws degree by Framingham State College in 1975; named honorary fellow by Ontario College of Art in 1975; nominated in 1977 by the National Cartoonists Society as the year's outstanding editorial cartoonist.

1977 PULITZER PRIZE

'I'll be Jack Kennedy . . . Who do you want to be?'

1976 SIGMA DELTA CHI AWARD
(Selected in 1977)

'MY FIRST PROMISE IS TO BREAK MY EARLIER PROMISE NOT TO RUN FOR OFFICE.'

1977 NATIONAL HEADLINERS CLUB AWARD

"FILL 'ER UP!"

1976 NATIONAL NEWSPAPER AWARD/CANADA
(Selected in 1977)

ANDY DONATO
Editorial Cartoonist
Toronto Sun

Born in Toronto, Canada, in 1938; joined the *Toronto Telegram* as a promotional artist; began drawing political cartoons in 1965; joined the *Toronto Sun* as editorial cartoonist in 1971; sculptor, waterpainter, lampmaker; author of *The Best of Donato*, a collection of his works.

Best Editorial Cartoons of the Year

Carter Administration

Many politicians agreed that the reason President Carter's programs ran into so much trouble during his first year in office was because he tried to do too much.

For example, his plan for a $50 tax rebate to taxpayers suffered rough going, and he quickly abandoned the idea. Congress would not approve Carter's gasoline tax, but did pass his proposal to tax "gas guzzlers." The president wanted 18 major water projects halted, but Congress trimmed less than half.

Carter's consumer agency proposal was stalled, as was his plan to abolish the electoral college. He also wanted to halt construction of the Clinch River, Tennessee, breeder reactor because of environmental concerns, but Congress voted to continue the project. Carter nevertheless vetoed the authorization bill in November.

Carter pushed hard for one pet project, instant voter registration, but again Congress balked. Human rights was the centerpiece of the president's foreign policy but as the year wore on he toned down his advocacy of individual liberty and support of dissidents in the Soviet Union. The fate of the Panama Canal treaty, one of Carter's top priorities, remained uncertain at year's end. Carter's pardoning of Vietnam-era draft dodgers and his ordered withdrawal of U.S. ground troops from South Korea within five years drew mixed support.

JEFF MACNELLY
Richmond News Leader
©Chicago Tribune—New York News Syndicate

TOM CURTIS
Courtesy Milwaukee Sentinel

"This inauguration ceremony marks a new beginning..."

ANDY DONATO
Courtesy Toronto Sun

JACK McLEOD
Courtesy Buffalo Evening News

... AND EVERYWHERE THAT JIMMY WENT...

HUGH HAYNIE
Louisville Courier-Journal
©Los Angeles Times Syndicate

'...and for heaven's sake, Jimmy, quit using that Southern accent. We're on holiday!'

BEN WICKS
Courtesy Toronto Sun

CHARLES WERNER
Courtesy Indianapolis Star

BERT WHITMAN
Courtesy Phoenix Gazette

FIRST FIRESIDE CHAT

MERLE CUNNINGTON
Courtesy Valley News (Calif.)

DAN LYNCH
Courtesy Ft. Wayne Journal-Gazette

ED VALTMAN
©Rothco

'WE OBSERVE IN SORROW HIS UNTIMELY PASSING. BUT HIS SHORT LIFE WAS FULL OF PROMISE AND FILLED OUR HEARTS WITH HOPE'

"Are there any new ideas for symbolic gestures?"

"Mah frans..."

DRESS FOR FUTURE CHATS: FARM PROGRAM, LABOR RELATIONS AND DEFENSE POLICY....

WAYNE STAYSKAL
Courtesy Chicago Tribune

"SEEMS LIKE ONLY YESTERDAY THAT I STOOD RIGHT HERE AND BURNED MY DRAFT CARD!"

BILL DE ORE
Courtesy Dallas Morning News

JOHN RIEDELL
Courtesy Peoria Journal

ART WOOD
Courtesy U. S. Independent Telephone Assn.

DON HESSE
Courtesy St. Louis Globe-Democrat

ED GAMBLE
Courtesy Nashville Banner

A MESS

VERN THOMPSON
Courtesy Lawton (Okla.) Constitution

CAESAR TOO, WAS AMBITIOUS!

JOHN MILT MORRIS
©The Associated Press

BOB ENGLEHART
Courtesy Dayton Journal Herald
Copley News Service

"LIFE IS UNFAIR."

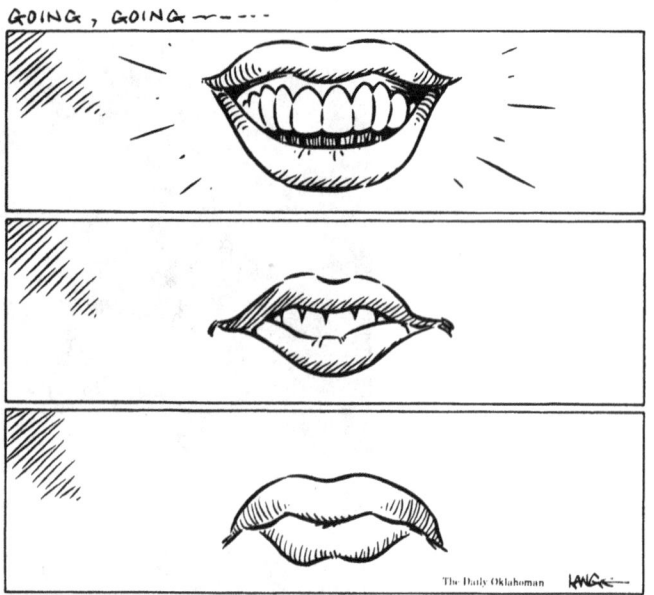

JIM LANGE
The Daily Oklahoman
©The Oklahoma Publishing Co.

BOB SULLIVAN
Courtesy Worcester (Mass.) Telegram

1976 — The Making of a President — 1977

Bert Lance

Bert Lance, Director of the Office of Management and Budget and a Carter crony from Georgia, became the first casualty of the post-Watergate focus on ethical conduct on September 21 when Carter announced his friend's resignation. Lance, a banker and wheeler dealer, had been in the headlines for months because of alleged improprieties while president of the Calhoun First National Bank and the National Bank of Georgia. Allegations against Lance were investigated by a variety of government agencies, and Lance offered answers in three days of hearings conducted by the Senate Governmental Affairs Committee.

His critics remained unconvinced, however. Carter, who had praised Lance in glowing terms earlier, finally had to act and accepted his resignation.

BOB TAYLOR
Courtesy Dallas Times Herald

RAY OSRIN
Courtesy Cleveland Plain Dealer

HY ROSEN
Courtesy Albany Times-Union

S. C. RAWLS
Courtesy Palm Beach Post

PAUL SZEP
Courtesy Boston Globe

"I AM NOT A CROOK... I'M A BANKER"

"I guess I never noticed it before."

JOHN LANE
©NEA

CHARLES DANIEL
Courtesy Knoxville Journal

MIKE KEEFE
Courtesy Denver Post

ETTA HULME
Courtesy Ft. Worth Star-Telegram

TOM ENGELHARDT
Courtesy St. Louis Post-Dispatch

'. . . But It Doesn't Do Much For The Image Of The Preacher'

JIM BORGMAN
Courtesy Cincinnati Enquirer

ROY PETERSON
Courtesy Vancouver Sun

ANDY DONATO
Courtesy Toronto Sun

CLYDE WELLS
Courtesy Augusta (Ga.) Chronicle

JOHN FISCHETTI
Courtesy Chicago Daily News

"IT'S SENATOR PERCY — HE SAYS MY ACCOUNT IS OVERDRAWN"

DAN LYNCH
Courtesy Ft. Wayne Journal-Gazette

"AWRIGHT NOBODY MOVE! THIS IS AN OVERDRAFT!"

ALL WASHED UP!

ROB LAWLOR
Courtesy Philadelphia Daily News

TIM MENEES
Courtesy Pittsburgh Post-Gazette

'I shot a Lance into the air...'

BOB ARTLEY
Courtesy Worthington (Minn.) Daily Globe

CHARLES WERNER
Courtesy Indianapolis Star

KATE PALMER
Courtesy Greenville (S.C.) News

BILL DE ORE
Courtesy Dallas Morning News

Andrew Young

Shortly after the Carter Administration took office, Andrew Young, the new chief U.S. delegate to the United Nations, established a reputation as the most controversial member of Carter's team.

Young made three trips to Africa and apparently assisted in formulating U.S. policy in that troubled part of the world. It was not his diplomacy, however, that made the biggest news. His strong, direct, and often intemperate remarks about various subjects—and governments—created a furor at home and abroad.

He announced, for example, that the presence of Cuban troops in Angola could help stabilize the region, an opinion quickly disavowed by the U.S. State Department. He later proclaimed that the Russians were the worst racists in the world, and that when the crunch comes, the black in Sweden is treated as unjustly as the black in Queens, New York.

Still later, Young referred to former presidents Richard Nixon and Gerald Ford as racists.

Calls for Young's resignation were made from various quarters, but they went unheeded.

LEN BOROZWSKI
Courtesy San Diego Union

CARL LARSEN
Courtesy Richmond Times-Dispatch

BLUNDERBUSS

KARL HUBENTHAL
Courtesy Los Angeles
Herald-Examiner

'AMBASSADOR YOUNG, THE PRESIDENT WILL SEE YOU NOW'

CRAIG MACINTOSH
Courtesy Minneapolis Star

CARTER'S "OPEN" FOREIGN POLICY

The world of Andrew Young

RICKY NOBILE
Courtesy Bolivar (Miss.) Commercial

REG MANNING
Courtesy Arizona Republic

JIM BORGMAN
Courtesy Cincinnati Enquirer

JERRY ROBINSON
©Chicago Tribune-N.Y. News Syndicate

WAYNE STAYSKAL
Courtesy Chicago Tribune

"I WISH THEY WOULD GO BACK TO BEATING THEIR DRUMS... THAT CONSTANT SINGING OF 'WE SHALL OVERCOME' IS DRIVING ME BATS!"

Korean Scandal

Congress seemed in no great hurry to dig into persistent rumors about a Korean bribery scandal, but in August the Justice Department finally blew the lid off. Attorney General Griffin Bell announced the indictment of Tongsun Park, a South Korean businessman, by a federal grand jury.

Park, widely known in Washington, was accused of being a secret agent of the South Korean government and of trying to influence Congressmen with gifts, junkets, parties, and cash. Park insisted that whatever he did in Washington was done on his own initiative. The South Korean government also denied any responsibility for Park's dealings. Leon Jaworski, the former Watergate prosecutor, was named to head up an inquiry.

After lengthy negotiations with the South Korean government and much pressure from Washington, Park finally agreed to return to the U.S. to answer the charges in court—but not before the Jaworski committee. The grand jury indictment of Park named 11 present members of Congress and 13 former members as recipients of cash gifts or campaign contributions from Park. At year's end, however, Congress had taken no action against any of the lawmakers allegedly receiving Park's cash favors.

MIKE KEEFE
Courtesy Denver Post

'WE KNOW YOU'RE IN THERE, PARK... PLEASE, DON'T COME OUT!'

GENE BASSET
Courtesy Scripps-Howard Newspapers

"THAT KOREAN HAD HIS NERVE TRYING TO BUY INFLUENCE ON CAPITOL HILL"

DICK WRIGHT
Courtesy Providence Journal-Bulletin

HOT ON THE TRAIL!

BILL GRAHAM
Courtesy Arkansas Gazette

JOHN SHEVCHIK
*Courtesy Beaver Falls (Pa.)
News Tribune*

"We are not a crook!"

HERC FICKLEN
©Avalon Features

ERIC SMITH
Courtesy Capital-Gazette (Md.) Newspapers

ART HENRIKSON
Courtesy Des Plaines (Ill.) Herald

TOM ENGELHARDT
Courtesy St. Louis Post-Dispatch

I say let's get on with it. Indictment, prison, release, talk shows, books, royalties . . .

'No, No, Boy—Koreans, Remember?'

ED FISCHER
Courtesy Omaha World-Herald

41

EUGENE CRAIG
Courtesy Columbus (O.) Dispatch

ART BIMROSE
Courtesy Portland Oregonian

JIM MORIN
Courtesy Richmond Times-Dispatch

Congress

Although a Democratic president held forth in the White House and the Democrats controlled Congress, 1977 was hardly a smooth-sailing year for Carter. An independent-minded Congress demonstrated it would not follow any president blindly. The clash started even before Carter was sworn in when Theodore Sorenson, Carter's first choice for CIA director, ran into so much opposition in the Senate that he withdrew his name.

The president's energy bill was so battered that, when finally approved in 1978, it will fall far short of what Carter wanted. His tax increases have been replaced with billions in new tax breaks for businessmen and others. There seemed to be a strong feeling among veteran Congressmen that Congress had yielded too much power to the Executive Branch—and it was therefore time to assert themselves. In addition, new members of Congress have weak ties with their party and are less inclined to follow party dictates.

In any event, Congress was up to one of its old tricks during the year—spending money wildly. It approved a new Department of Energy that will cost billions of dollars annually and voted Congressmen a $12,900 annual pay increase. In the final bill increasing price supports for wheat, grain, and cotton, Congress even voted $1 billion more than Carter had asked.

BILL GARNER
Courtesy The Commercial Appeal

JIM BERRY
©NEA

"OK! If Jimmy Carter wants to go over our heads by appealing directly to the people — WE can play dirty, too!"

DENNIS RENAULT
Courtesy Sacremento Bee

'I pledge allegiance to the Oil Lobby of America and to the Corporations for which it stands. One Industry, uncontrolled, indivisible with Liberty to rip off us All.'

OLLIE HARRINGTON
Courtesy New York Daily World

"JUST KEEP SHOUTIN' 'HUMAN RIGHTS,' SENATOR, AND WE'LL DO THE REST."

DON HESSE
Courtesy St. Louis Globe-Democrat

"THINGS ARE REALLY GETTING TOUGH. FOOD COSTS RISING, MEDICAL COSTS UP, HOUSING SKYROCKETING..."

"...AND NOW THE HIGH COST OF HEATING FUEL! IT'S TIME WE DID SOMETHING ABOUT IT!"

"ALL THOSE IN FAVOR OF A $12,900 RAISE SAY 'AYE'."

"aye."

DICK WRIGHT
Courtesy Providence Journal-Bulletin

DAVID SEAVEY
©National Observer

FRANK INTERLANDI
©Los Angeles Times Syndicate

BEN WICKS
Courtesy Toronto Sun

"Looks like an oil spill to me!"

'It's Congress. They've got Amy!'

JACK BENDER
Waterloo Courier
©Rothco Cartoons, Inc.

LARRY WRIGHT
Courtesy Detroit News

OLLIE HARRINGTON
Courtesy New York Daily World

"Bring it past the Senate windows; they're discussing the military budget."

GEORGE FISHER
Courtesy Arkansas Gazette

The Economy

The nation's economy failed to boom during 1977 as the Carter Administration had hoped. In fact, the business outlook grew cloudier. Investors held back money and, in general, confidence throughout the U.S. business community sagged.

Throughout the year a slumping stock market caused concern. Business found it difficult to raise money for expansion and modernization. U.S. dependence on imported oil continued to grow, and the foreign trade deficit rose to a record high—some $25 billion for the year. In an effort to stimulate employment, Carter pushed through legislation to prime the pump—$4 billion for public works and $7.9 billion for public service jobholders. The unemployment rate dropped slightly from 7.3 percent to 6.9 percent.

The dollar took a battering in foreign exchange markets, particularly against the West German mark, the Japanese yen, and the Swiss franc. Inflation hovered at around 6 percent, and wage earners were hard-pressed to keep pace with the cost of living. Farmers threatened to go on strike to boost prices, and the steel industry was hit hard from two directions—competition from foreign markets and increased costs as a result of stiffer environmental standards and regulations.

CHARLES BROOKS
Courtesy Birmingham (Ala.) News

MODERN ECONOMICS

The difference between unemployment during a Republican administration and a Democratic administration!

"YESSIR... SOUND AS A DOLLAR!"

"I WISH YOU HADN'T SAID THAT, DOC!"

TOM CURTIS
Courtesy Milwaukee Sentinel

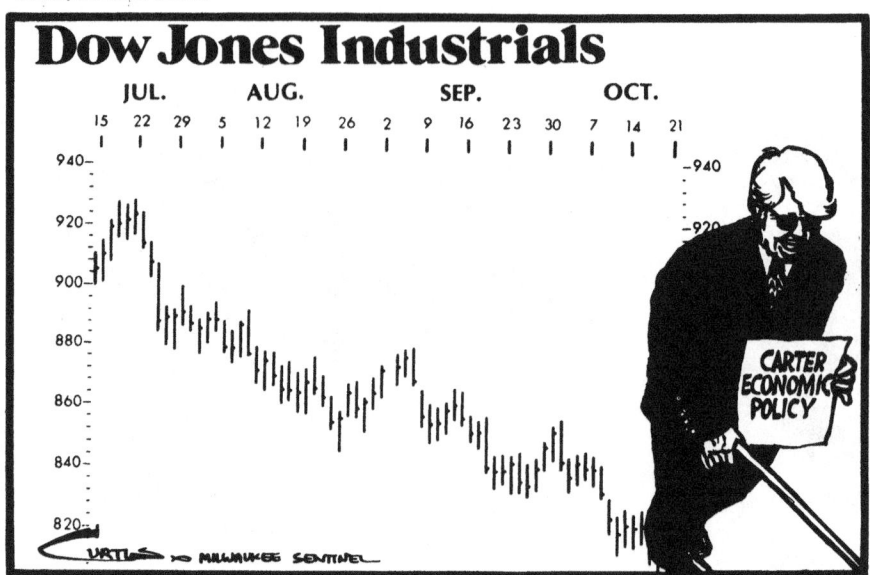

DON HESSE
Courtesy St. Louis Globe-Democrat

'I'M TRYING TO KEEP HIM ON HIS FEET'

BILL DAY
Courtesy Oakland Press

TOM FLANNERY
Courtesy Baltimore Sun

The American Dream House

ED ULUSCHAK
Courtesy Edmonton (Can.) Journal

"Because we're boycotting coffee, that's why — now stop griping and drink your hot water!"

DOUG SNEYD
Courtesy Toronto Star

"There's a small change in the heist. Instead of going for the bank, we hit the coffee warehouse next door to it."

JIM IVEY
Orlando Sentinel Star
©Rothco Cartoons, Inc.

RAY OSRIN
Courtesy Cleveland Plain Dealer

BEN SARGENT
Courtesy Austin American

ED FISCHER
Courtesy Omaha World-Herald

AMERICAN GOTHIC

CHARLES BROOKS
Courtesy Birmingham (Ala.) News

CLYDE PETERSON
Courtesy Houston Chronicle

'GO AHEAD AND OPERATE. JUST DON'T DRAW BLOOD!'

SCOTT LONG
Courtesy Minneapolis Tribune

DICK LOCHER
Courtesy Chicago Tribune

AL LIEDERMAN
Courtesy Long Island Press

BEN SARGENT
Courtesy Austin American

CLYDE PETERSON
Courtesy Houston Chronicle

'And then we have our styrofoam shell option for those who can't kick the big car habit cold turkey'

Foreign Relations

U.S. relations with Peking were cordial throughout the year. The Chinese, however, expressed concern after Secretary of State Cyrus Vance returned from the mainland and it was reported that he found flexibility in China's position on normalization of relations. Vice-premier Teng Hsiao-ping strongly denied any change in the Chinese position. Peking still insists on U.S. derecognition of the Taiwan government, removal of American troops, and abrogation of the existing defense treaty.

After 18 years of strained relations, the Carter Administration agreed to exchange diplomats with Cuba. The president made it clear that the U.S. is now officially willing to deal with political systems that are dictatorial and communist. South Africa and Rhodesia were the targets of increased diplomatic activity during the year. Compromise settlements offered by Ian Smith's white government on the question of majority rule in Rhodesia were rejected. Drug traffic between Mexico and the U.S. remained a serious problem, as did the growing flood of Mexicans who entered the U.S. illegally in search of jobs.

Russian leaders were annoyed by President Carter's stand on human rights, a factor that contributed to the deadlocked SALT talks.

JIM MORIN
*Courtesy Beaumont
Enterprise and Journal*

GEORGE FISHER
Courtesy Arkansas Gazette

"Gee, and just when I thought I was getting the hang of it."

REALISM...

DRAPER HILL
Courtesy Detroit News

ALBERTO HUICI
Courtesy Jueves de Excelsior (Mex.)

KEVIN McVEY
Courtesy The Record, Hackensack, N. J.

FRANK INTERLANDI
©Los Angeles Times Syndicate

Castro makes Overtures!

ART HENRIKSON
Courtesy Des Plaines (Ill.) Herald

Sure you recognize him. I do!

DON HESSE
Courtesy St. Louis Globe-Democrat

JIM KNUDSEN
Courtesy N.Y. Catholic News

DOUG SNEYD
Courtesy Toronto Star

"Dear President Carter: Thank you for your letter of concern which was forwarded to me here at this beautiful Black Sea Resort..."

TIM MENEES
Courtesy Pittsburgh Post-Gazette

DENNIS RENAULT
Courtesy Sacremento Bee

TOM ENGELHARDT
Courtesy St. Louis Post-Dispatch

'Tell me, how are things in the Free World?'

'You're Under Arrest, Comrade, For Trying To Melt Down This Monument'

'WE DON'T ARREST PEOPLE – WE HOSPITALIZE THEM'

ED VALTMAN
©Rothco

CHARLES BROOKS
Courtesy Birmingham (Ala.) News

TIM MENEES
Courtesy Pittsburgh
Post-Gazette

ANTHONY JENKINS
Courtesy Toronto Globe and Mail

KEN WESTPHAL
Courtesy Wichita Eagle

JACK McLEOD
Courtesy Buffalo Evening News

BOB SULLIVAN
Courtesy Worcester (Mass.) Telegram

INDIA'S DEMOCRACY IN ACTION

Human Rights

Before the U.S. Supreme Court adjourns in mid-1978, that body probably will have acted on at least 60 cases involving individual rights. One case on which a great deal of attention has focused is a suit brought by 37-year-old Allan Bakke, who was denied admission as a medical student at the University of California. Bakke claimed he was the victim of illegal racial discrimination because the university had reserved 16 spaces in its freshman medical school class for minorities. Bakke argued that the 16 were less qualified than he.

Congress passed legislation making it illegal to force a worker from his job at age 65. Many saw this as the first step toward abolishing compulsory retirement in private industry.

Foreign governments reacted strongly during the year to President Carter's aggressive stand on human rights, viewing his statements as interference in their domestic affairs.

Women made headlines with the human rights issue. A federally funded National Women's Conference was held in Houston, generating a great deal of rhetoric. Anita Bryant led a campaign in Miami to repeal an ordinance that prohibited discrimination against homosexuals. Her campaign was successful, but she contended her stand cost her some bookings.

JIM DOBBINS
Courtesy Manchester Union-Leader

Roots

JACK BENDER
Waterloo Courier
©Rothco Cartoons, Inc.

ED GAMBLE
Courtesy Nashville Banner

"GOOD NEWS... WE'VE DECIDED TO EXTEND THE FIGHT UNTIL YOU WIN!"

ETTA HULME
Courtesy Ft. Worth Star-Telegram

"I SHOULD THINK YOU'D APPRECIATE THE WAY WE ALWAYS PUT YOU ON A PEDESTAL"

GENE BASSET
Courtesy Scripps-Howard Newspapers

THE JUDGMENT OF SOLOMON

DRAPER HILL
Courtesy Detroit News

WILLIAM SOLANO
Courtesy La Nacion, San Jose, Costa Rica

CHARLES BISSELL
Courtesy Nashville Tennessean

'Human Rights?... Mind You Own Business!'

BALDY
Courtesy Atlanta Constitution

'...Can't You Waffle Again?'

GUERNSEY LEPELLEY
Courtesy Christian Science Monitor

"But every time I take you to a nice party, you bite somebody."

KATE PALMER
Courtesy Greenville (S.C.) News

JOHN LANE
©NEA

ART BIMROSE
Courtesy Portland Oregonian

HEAT AND LIGHT

FRANK WILLIAMS
Courtesy Detroit Free-Press

THE ROSE GREW THORNS

"Carter's Moral Crusade"

REG MANNING
Courtesy Arizona Republic

VERN THOMPSON
Courtesy Lawton (Okla.) Constitution

The Middle East

America's role in the Middle East negotiations changed somewhat after Egypt's President Anwar Sadat took the initiative with his dramatic trip to Jerusalem. But while Egyptians and Israelis negotiated face to face in an unprecedented series of meetings, the U.S. nevertheless was counted on heavily to make decisive contributions toward a lasting peace.

At year's end, two major stumbling blocks seemed to stand in the way of a settlement: self-determination for the Palestinians and recovery by Egypt of lands captured by Israel in previous wars.

"...HOW LONG WOULD IT TAKE TO TURN IT AROUND?"

BALDY
Courtesy Atlanta Constitution

JERRY ROBINSON
©Chicago Tribune-N.Y. News Syndicate

BOB ENGLEHART
Courtesy Dayton Journal Herald

BOB ARTLEY
Courtesy Worthington (Minn.) Daily Globe

JEFF MACNELLY
Richmond News Leader
©Chicago Tribune—New York News Syndicate

VIC ROSCHKOV
Courtesy Toronto Star

SPEAKING THE SAME LANGUAGE

KARL HUBENTHAL
Courtesy Los Angeles
Herald-Examiner

BYRON HUMPHREY
Courtesy New Orleans States-Item

DICK WRIGHT
Courtesy Providence
Journal-Bulletin

RAY OSRIN
Courtesy Cleveland Plain Dealer

STAR WARS

JERRY BITTLE
Courtesy Albuquerque Tribune

"It says, 'Negotiations between Israelites, Egyptians, and Philistines are proceeding slowly.'"

GUERNSEY LEPELLEY
Courtesy Christian Science Monitor

BILL ANDREWS
Courtesy New York Daily World

FRANK SPANGLER
*Courtesy Montgomery (Ala.)
Advertiser*

JOHN TREVER
*Courtesy Albuquerque
Journal*

DWANE POWELL
Courtesy News and Observer

BILL GARNER
Courtesy The Commercial Appeal

Panama Canal

With great pomp and ceremony, President Carter on September 7 signed treaties with Panama strongman General Omar Torrijos which, if ratified, would deliver the canal to the tiny Latin American country by the end of this century. Even as the treaties were being signed, however, opponents of the move were loudly registering their disapproval.

Under the U.S. Constitution, a treaty must be ratified by two-thirds of the Senate present and voting. At the time of the signing, at least 30 senators indicated they either were opposed to or inclined to oppose the treaties. Former President Gerald Ford and former Secretary of State Henry Kissinger lined up in favor of the treaties, while former California Governor Ronald Reagan headed a list of opponents.

Under a separate understanding, the U.S. also agreed to give Panama $345 million in economic and military aid over the next several years, as well as to increase payments for the use of the canal from $2.3 million annually to about $60 million a year.

In the October balloting, the citizens of Panama approved the treaties by a two-to-one margin. Polls in late 1977 showed strong sentiment in the U.S. against giving up the canal.

HUGH HAYNIE
Louisville Courier-Journal
©Los Angeles Times Syndicate

After signing the historic document, Gen. Torrijos hands it to Pres. Carter.

The President signs it and passes it to the Senate for ratification.

The Senate, in turn, places it under consideration.

BOB TAYLOR
Courtesy Dallas Times Herald

EDDIE GERMANO
Courtesy Brockton Daily Enterprise

SANDY CAMPBELL
Courtesy The Tennessean

FIDDLER ON THE ROOF

'SMILE when you say that, Hombre'

DAVID SEAVEY
©National Observer

ELDON PLETCHER
Courtesy New Orleans Times-Picayune

"THE PANAMA CANAL TREATY"

HAROLD MAPLES
Courtesy Ft. Worth Star-Telegram

JOHN STAMPONE
Courtesy Army Times

DICK WALLMEYER
Long Beach Press-Telegram
©Register and Tribune Syndicate

"GET ME OMAR TORRIJOS' LAWYER!"

HY ROSEN
Courtesy Albany Times-Union

"I GOT MY HALF, GRINGO!"

"Hold onto your hats, folks!"

TOM CURTIS
Courtesy Milwaukee Sentinel

Hot on his heels

PAP DEAN
Courtesy Shreveport Times

"It's your swimming pool, but it's our shark."

GUERNSEY LEPELLEY
Courtesy Christian Science Monitor

Africa

The African continent continued as a center of seething unrest throughout 1977. Ethiopia, fighting for survival against internal dissidents, now relies almost solely on Russian support. On June 27, the last French colony on mainland Africa gained independence as the Republic of Djibouti, but its political and economic future remained tenuous. In Kenya, factions maneuvered for power as the aging President Kenyatta seemed near the end of his reign.

Russia made a strong bid for dominance in the strategic Horn of Africa, but Ethiopia and Somalia, both friendly toward the Soviet Union, fought continuing skirmishes. The leftist regime of Sudan rejected Moscow and looked toward the U.S. for aid.

President Carter pressed hard for social change in white-controlled South Africa, but one immediate effect was to drive many moderate South Africans toward a more "hard line" stance. In Rhodesia, Prime Minister Ian Smith rejected various proposals based on "one man, one vote," contending that no safeguards for Rhodesian whites had been devised.

Ugandan President Idi Amin Dada continued to wage a bloodbath against his political enemies. Ugandan refugees who fled to Kenya after an unsuccessful coup attempt against the dictator told appalling stories of bloody reprisals.

VIC ROSCHKOV
Courtesy Toronto Star

THE GROWTH

"The real trick is how do we stop him from thinking....?"

S. C. RAWLS
Courtesy Palm Beach Post

"No, no, no. . . . You, Jane, <u>ME</u> Tarzan."

GUERNSEY LEPELLEY
Courtesy Christian Science Monitor

Timber..r..r..r'

LEW HARSH
Courtesy Scranton Times

KEN WESTPHAL
Courtesy Wichita Eagle

DICK WALLMEYER
Long Beach Press-Telegram
©Register and Tribune Syndicate

Odd couple

VIC RUNTZ
Courtesy Bangor Daily News

EDD ULUSCHAK
Courtesy Edmonton Journal

"Okay — come on out with your hands up!"

VERN THOMPSON
Courtesy Lawton (Okla.) Constitution

MERLE TINGLEY
Courtesy London (Can.) Free Press

FRANK INTERLANDI
©Los Angeles Times Syndicate

DANI AGUILA
Courtesy Filipino Reporter

CHARLES WERNER
Courtesy Indianapolis Star

DWANE POWELL
Courtesy News and Observer

KEN ALEXANDER
Courtesy San Francisco Examiner

"Crazy, man"

Alaskan Pipeline

On July 28, the new 800-mile long Alaskan pipeline delivered its first crude oil from the barren North Slope at Prudhoe Bay to the Valdez tanker terminal. Construction of the pipeline was the largest private project ever undertaken in peacetime. Beginning above the Arctic Circle, it snakes southward over three mountain ranges, tunnels under 70 rivers and streams, and spans 50 others, ending at the ice-free port of Valdez. The 48-inch diameter, all-welded steel pipeline required the efforts of 21,000 laborers.

Serious problems surfaced almost immediately after construction was completed. A liquid nitrogen leak under repair led to an explosion which killed one workman. In addition, a major question loomed concerning how to transport the oil cheaply to refineries. It had been assumed that large tankers would carry the oil from Valdez to West Coast ports, but many ports would not allow the tankers to dock because of environmental concerns. Furthermore, the largest, most economical tankers were too large to sail through the Panama Canal.

JIM BORGMAN
Courtesy Cincinnati Enquirer

MIKE KEEFE
Courtesy Denver Post

"Human failure, mechanical failure, it's still oil and it still tastes like hell."

KEN ALEXANDER
Courtesy San Francisco Examiner

JIMMY MARGULIES
©Rothco Cartoons

JAMES MORGAN
Courtesy Spartanburg Herald-Journal

AURORA DOLLARALIS

LEE JUDGE
Sacramento Union
©Lee Judge Syndicate

Energy

Petroleum imports rose sharply during the year as consumer demand for gasoline maintained its record pace. The oil imports were the main reason for a projected annual trade deficit of some $25 billion—four times as large as any previous figure. In an effort to reduce the need for imported oil, President Carter proposed a 50 percent increase in the use of coal by 1985. Many plants were in the process of converting from electricity and gas to coal.

Carter Administration projections indicate that if energy consumption continues at its present rate, U.S. demand will exceed the known world reserves by 1985. Some experts, however, doubt such an assessment. Government and private business interests have expanded their search for new energy sources and are studying the possibility of tapping geothermal energy, or underground heat. Six cities in Iceland have been heated by this type of energy for many years. Highway motorists gave little evidence of being concerned about conserving energy. In most states, drivers ignored the 55-mile-per-hour speed limit and drove much as they did before the Arab oil embargo.

HUGH HAYNIE
Louisville Courier-Journal
©Los Angeles Times Syndicate

TOM ENGELHARDT
Courtesy St. Louis Post-Dispatch

"IT'S THE STATE P.U.C. ... SHOULD I TELL THEM THE ONE ABOUT THE NEXT THREE QUARTERS POSSIBLY NOT BEING AS PROFITABLE AS THIS ONE WAS?"

BOB BECKETT
Courtesy Burlington County (N.J.) Times

GENE BASSET
Courtesy Scripps-Howard Newspapers

BOB ENGLEHART
Courtesy Dayton Journal Herald

"WHAT HAVE YOU GOT THAT'LL GIVE ME GAS?"

RAY OSRIN
Courtesy Cleveland Plain Dealer

SELECTING A COFFIN

SCOTT LONG
Courtesy Minneapolis Tribune

BOWLING FOR DOLLARS

BLAINE
Courtesy The Spectator, Canada

BILL GARNER
Courtesy The Commercial Appeal

ED FISCHER
Courtesy Omaha World-Herald

MERLE CUNNINGTON
Courtesy Valley News (Calif.)

"Which would you like first, the report on the economy or the weather?"

JIM BERRY
©NEA

CHARLES DANIEL
Courtesy Knoxville Journal

THINK ABOUT IT NEXT TIME YOU 'FILLER UP'!

JOHN MILT MORRIS
©The Associated Press

STEVE BRODNER
Courtesy Union City (N.J.) Dispatch

Leif Ericson Discovers The ~~New~~ Modern World

SANDY CAMPBELL
Courtesy The Tennessean

"THIS MIGHT TAKE AWHILE"

BILL CRAWFORD
©NEA

JERRY DOYLE
Courtesy Philadelphia Daily News

JERRY FEARING
Courtesy St. Paul Dispatch

DICK WALLMEYER
Long Beach Press-Telegram
©Register and Tribune Syndicate

MUST READING

BOOM TOWN

FRANK WILLIAMS
Courtesy Detroit Free-Press

JIM PALMER
Courtesy Dallas News

LEONARD NORRIS
Courtesy Vancouver (Can.) Sun

"True, she tends to get furious with my innovative energy conservation measures
... and that makes the light brighter."

DICK LOCHER
Courtesy Chicago Tribune

ART POINIER
© United Feature Syndicate

CHARLES WERNER
Courtesy Indianapolis Star

JERRY FEARING
Courtesy St. Paul Dispatch

U.S. Defense

The Soviet Union turned to outer space during the year in a strong effort to move ahead of the U.S. in the arms race. Secretary of Defense Harold Brown officially disclosed that the Russians had developed the operational capability to destroy American satellites.

In an effort to prevent a full-scale arms race in space, President Carter proposed a new U.S.-Russian agreement that would ban further experiments with killer satellites. The Soviets, however, were unreceptive to the idea.

U.S. development of the neutron bomb generated a wealth of controversy, both at home and abroad. The weapon was designed specifically as a deterrent to a possible attack by Soviet tanks across Central Europe. Because of its strong radiation yield and restricted blast power, the weapon can kill while leaving buildings and equipment intact.

President Carter's June 30 decision not to proceed with production of the B-1 bomber set off loud arguments across the country. His announcement meant the U.S. would have to rely heavily on refurbished B-52s built decades ago. Carter proposed the accelerated development of the cruise missile, a relatively cheap and highly accurate supersonic weapon. He also pushed hard for a SALT agreement with the Soviets, and announced hopes for signing an agreement in 1978.

DEVOLUTION

JOHN FISCHETTI
Courtesy Chicago Daily News

LARRY WRIGHT
Courtesy Detroit News

THE MISSING LINK*

*HE BELIEVED THE KREMLIN WOULD STOP ALL ATOMIC TESTING AND STOCKPILING!

JIM DOBBINS
Courtesy Manchester Union-Leader

PAUL SZEP
Courtesy Boston Globe

JOHN CRAWFORD
Courtesy Alabama Journal

OLLIE HARRINGTON
Courtesy New York Daily World

"LOOK ON THE BRIGHT SIDE _____ IT WONT DESTROY THE OFFICERS CLUB."

"My six-year-old grandson says if we bomb the species into extinction who's gonna enjoy all that untouched property. Cute, huh?"

MERLE TINGLEY
Courtesy London (Can.) Free Press

107

LOU ERICKSON
Courtesy Atlanta Journal

ED GAMBLE
Courtesy Nashville Banner

'Don't Give Me That Friend-Or-Foe Bit, Lower the Bridge'

JOHN STAMPONE
Courtesy Army Times

ETTA HULME
Courtesy Ft. Worth Star-Telegram

BILL ANDREWS
Courtesy New York Daily World

BILL ANDREWS
Courtesy New York Daily World

Another Energy Crisis

LEW HARSH
Courtesy Scranton Times

"Gentlemen, start your engines!"

BILL GRAHAM
Arkansas Gazette

Mac Carter

JIM DOBBINS
Courtesy Manchester Union-Leader

Terrorism

Terrorist violence continued throughout much of the world in 1977, with West Germany a frequent target. On October 18, commandoes stormed a hijacked West German airliner in Somalia, killing three of the hijackers and rescuing 86 hostages. The action apparently provoked a wave of retaliation by various left-wing groups, one of which murdered a kidnapped West German industrialist after demands for the release of imprisoned radicals were not met.

According to official reports, 27 deaths and 92 injuries have been caused in the past ten years by terrorism in West Germany. In addition, 100 hostages have been taken and 102 other persons have been the targets of attempted murder. Terrorism has become recognized as a growing danger in the U.S. Many corporations, for example, are now buying ransom insurance for key executives.

CLYDE PETERSON
Courtesy Houston Chronicle

'Why don't you call when you're bringing home hostages?'

BERT WHITMAN
Courtesy Phoenix Gazette

ROB LAWLOR
Courtesy Philadelphia Daily News

ART POINIER
© United Feature Syndicate

VERN THOMPSON
Courtesy Lawton (Okla.) Constitution

HY ROSEN
Courtesy Albany Times-Union

Richard Nixon

British television producer and performer David Frost made major news in 1977 when he aired a series of exclusive interviews with former President Richard M. Nixon. Frost questioned Nixon at great length on the subject of Watergate, much in the manner of a prosecutor in a court of law.

An estimated 45 million people across the U.S. watched the first interview, which dealt with Watergate. Nixon avoided any admission of having committed any criminal offenses in the matter, although he did acknowledge having made statements "that were not true."

According to reports, the former president was assured of $600,000 for the four ninety-minute interviews, plus a percentage of the profits. A fifth segment was shown on some stations later. The shows were taken from nearly 30 hours of interviews which Frost had taped with Nixon.

ANTHONY JENKINS
Courtesy Toronto Globe and Mail

HELLO, CHUCK? DICK. THE GONG SHOW, IT'S CUTTING INTO MY RATINGS. SEE WHAT YOU CAN GET ON THE PRODUCER... AND THAT BIONIC WOMAN; FIX HER WAGON TOO!

LOU GRANT
Oakland Tribune
©Los Angeles Times Syndicate

LEN BOROZWSKI
Courtesy San Diego Union

DRAPER HILL
Courtesy Detroit News

CLYDE PETERSON
Courtesy Houston Chronicle

ONE, FOR THE MONEY.....TWO, FOR THE SHOW

BLAINE
Courtesy The Spectator, Canada

'I'm not saying anything till I've talked to my lawyer and/or David Frost'

BILL GARNER
Courtesy The Commercial Appeal

"DEAR JOHN — IF IT WASN'T FOR MARTHA WE WOULDN'T BE IN THE FIX WE'RE IN"

NIXON COMES CLEAN

"I WASN'T A GOOD BUTCHER."

BOB TAYLOR
Courtesy Dallas Times Herald

THE PINOCCHIO INTERVIEWS

GENE BASSET
Courtesy Scripps-Howard Newspapers

Bureaucracy

President Carter's campaign promise to reduce bureaucracy in government received little attention in 1977 as the federal machine continued to proliferate. At year's end, there were 2.9 million civilian governmental employees on the payroll working out of more than 2,000 agencies, many of which had overlapping responsibilities. Waste, duplication, and foulups could be found throughout, and bosses often were powerless to fire the incompetents. A study showed that salaries and wages for federal civilian employees had risen from $7 billion in 1955 to $46.5 billion in 1977.

The paperwork burden of bureaucracy seemed to be a major culprit. Studies by one commission discovered that there are approximately 5,000 forms for public use by all agencies and a million forms for internal use. The Commission on Federal Paperwork reported that filling out forms requires the equivalent manpower of more than a million full-time employees.

The new Department of Energy, which President Carter proposed and Congress approved, was the first cabinet agency to be added in 11 years. It began operating October 1 with 20,000 employees and a budget of $10.6 billion.

KEN ALEXANDER
Courtesy San Francisco Examiner

"If made into paper it could supply the entire federal government for 16 minutes."

'I THINK THEY'RE STILL IN THERE SOMEWHERE'

ED ASHLEY
Courtesy Toledo Blade

LEW HARSH
Courtesy Scranton Times

Still Sloppin' the Hog!

ROBERT GRAYSMITH
Courtesy San Francisco Chronicle

"This is the President! Throw out your rubber stamps . . . I have you surrounded!"

BYRON HUMPHREY
Courtesy New Orleans States-Item

ROOTS

HAROLD MAPLES
Courtesy Ft. Worth Star-Telegram

Billy Carter

Capitalizing on his familial relationship to the president, Billy Carter, Jimmy's brother, reportedly earned at least $500,000 during 1977, a performance that raised more than a few eyebrows. The colorful, brash, outspoken Billy made personal appearances throughout the country, posing with beauty queens, offering his own brand of homespun philosophy, and even attending the world belly-flop contest in Vancouver.

Critics accused him of profiteering on the presidency, but unflappable Billy merely shrugged off their complaints.

His service station in Plains, Georgia, also saw boom times as tourists flocked to catch a glimpse of the president's brother. Billy reported his station was selling 2,000 cases of beer a month and would gross at least half a million dollars for the year.

Fond of beer and photographed across the country with a can in hand, Billy finally had a beer named after him. Billy Beer went on the market in many states, complete with his likeness on the can.

CLYDE WELLS
Courtesy Augusta (Ga.) Chronicle

LARRY WRIGHT
Courtesy Detroit News

JON KENNEDY
Courtesy Arkansas Democrat

FRANK SPANGLER
*Courtesy Montgomery (Ala.)
Advertiser*

'This stuff is peanuts!'

BALDY
Courtesy Atlanta Constitution

'...I See It Don't Do Much for You Either, Deacon!'

The Quebec Question

In Canada, increased priorities were given to federal-provincial relations in 1977 with the election of Rene Levesque's separatist party in Quebec. Levesque offered a proposal that a politically independent Quebec be allowed to have only an economic association with Canada, but the premiers of Canada's four western provinces turned the plan down.

A majority of polls have shown that independence for Quebec is still strongly opposed, even among the French-speaking population. Nevertheless, separatist sentiment for Quebec, the second most populous province in Canada, has grown steadily since the early 1960s. No one could be sure, however, whether an independent province could survive. Because of the separatist movement, new businesses seemed less inclined to move in, and the home offices of many large companies talked of leaving Quebec.

The continuing question of separation was much on the minds of Canadians as the year drew to a close.

EDD ULUSCHAK
Courtesy Edmonton Journal

"Is Canada still here?"

ANDY DONATO
Courtesy Toronto Sun

JOHN COLLINS
Courtesy Montreal (Can.) Gazette

CHARLES BISSELL
Courtesy Nashville Tennessean

VIC ROSCHKOV
Courtesy Toronto Star

The Canadianese Twins

ROY PETERSON
Courtesy Vancouver Sun

JOHN COLLINS
Courtesy Montreal (Can.) Gazette

SAWING A NATION IN HALF

BLAINE
Courtesy The Spectator, Canada

Pollution and Chemicals

Late in 1977, the U.S. Government decided to postpone for 18 months the Food and Drug Administration's proposed ban on the use of saccharin. Further studies of the artificial sweetener, as well as other food additives, were planned.

Oil spills continued to plague many coastal areas during the year. By the end of March, eight oil tankers had been lost. Half of the tankers lost the previous year had flown the Liberian flag. That country does not have the stiff regulations the U.S. requires, and it is believed that many American companies own these tankers because they can transport oil more cheaply.

The drug laetrile, used in some cancer treatments, became a controversial issue when it was banned by the Food and Drug Administration. The FDA maintained that laetrile has no medical value and could be dangerous to patients. The FDA brought an increasing number of health hazards to the public's attention—from substances being used in cosmetics to widely used drugs and foods. Many of these, the FDA said, could cause cancer, heart disease, or other serious ailments.

One of the year's major dilemmas remained unsolved: what to do with the vast amount of toxic waste that kept piling up.

ROB LAWLOR
Courtesy Philadelphia Daily News

The Blind Leading The Blind

DENNIS RENAULT
Courtesy Sacremento Bee

JOHN LANE
©NEA

IT ISN'T SANTA CLAUS!

ART POINIER
© United Feature Syndicate

CRAIG MACINTOSH
Courtesy Minneapolis Star

Hallowe'en is year-'round

VIC RUNTZ
Courtesy Bangor Daily News

LEONARD NORRIS
Courtesy Vancouver (Can.) Sun

"... and for being a nit and putting the thingamebob on upsidedown we're transferring you to Prudhoe Bay ..."

Education

Education faced mounting problems throughout 1977. Violence in schools and a lack of discipline continued to hold the spotlight. The U.S. Supreme Court ruled that spanking of unruly students was constitutional, but there was no rush in the schools to take advantage of the edict.

Achievements on Scholastic Aptitude Tests continued to drop, with much of the decline attributed to lower-scoring women students, the disadvantaged, and minorities. Since 1963, the mean for SAT scores has dropped 49 points on the verbal section of the test. Average scores for mathematics dropped 32 points during the same period.

Excessive television viewing was singled out in several studies as one of the major reasons youngsters are not learning. Textbooks have been made easier in recent years, while learning standards have been lowered and absenteeism is growing. An increase in broken homes and changing family patterns have contributed to the continuing decline in learning.

The permissive era of easy-to-get grades and guaranteed diplomas seemed to be on its way out as educators talked more and more of a return to basics.

ED GAMBLE
Courtesy Nashville Banner

BOB BECKETT
Courtesy Burlington County (N.J.) Times

CHESTER COMMODORE
Courtesy Chicago Daily Defender

"I'VE GOT A FEELING HE'S JUST WAITING FOR ME TO FOUL UP!"

WAYNE STAYSKAL
Courtesy Chicago Tribune

Modern Education

Crime

Criminal sentencing in the U.S. has been termed a national scandal, and Congress is considering laws aimed at making punishment for federal crimes both uniform and certain. In the past, critics say, too much discretion has been given to judges in sentencing. Different courtrooms impose widely differing sentences for similar crimes. Many Congressmen have announced their intentions to change this.

Public concern has grown in recent years because in too many cases convicted criminals are given probationary sentences for their first, second, and even third crimes—often serving no time in jail at all.

Arson has become the fastest-growing crime in the U.S., with property losses running into billions of dollars annually and personal injury and loss of life growing. In New York City, arson was suspected in more than half of the fires that destroy 300 to 400 buildings a month.

Attorney General Griffin Bell launched a drive during the year to prosecute FBI and CIA officers who broke the law while carrying out their duties. A deluge of mail protesting his plan seemed to give Bell second thoughts at year's end.

JON KENNEDY
Courtesy Arkansas Democrat

VIC CANTONE
Courtesy N.Y. Daily News

BILL DAY
Courtesy Oakland Press

LEE JUDGE
Sacremento Union
©Lee Judge Syndicate

VIC CANTONE
Courtesy N.Y. Daily News

CHESTER COMMODORE
Courtesy Chicago Daily Defender

ROBERT C. DREBELBIS
Courtesy Harrison (Ark.) Daily Times

JOHN CRAWFORD
Courtesy Alabama Journal

LOU GRANT
Oakland Tribune
©Los Angeles Times Syndicate

BLAINE
Courtesy The Spectator, Canada

KEN ALEXANDER
Courtesy San Francisco Examiner

"You haf ze wrong place . . . our contract wiz ze CIA expired weeks ago."

'There are only two problems...'

JIM ORTON
©Computer World

JON KENNEDY
Courtesy Arkansas Democrat

'If you ever expect to get out of here, say AH!'

MIKE KEEFE
Courtesy Denver Post

Social Security

By 1977, it had become increasingly apparent that unless drastic steps were taken soon, the nation's Social Security system would collapse. The economics simply did not add up. During the year, some $5.5 billion more was paid out in benefits than was collected in payroll taxes. For the past several years, Congress had simply been unwilling to face the problem squarely.

In the final days of the 1977 session, however, Congress finally decided to bite the bullet. As a result, Congress sent the White House a bill that will add $227 billion to Social Security taxes in the next decade. By 1986, the yearly Social Security tax burden will be $40 billion greater than it would have been under the old law.

It was hoped that this staggering tax boost will enable the system to remain solvent, at least until the year 2000, but this seems doubtful.

HECK OF A WAY TO RUN A RAILROAD

KARL HUBENTHAL
Courtesy Los Angeles
Herald-Examiner

BEN SARGENT
Courtesy Austin American

EUGENE CRAIG
Courtesy Columbus (O.) Dispatch

BALDY
Courtesy Atlanta Constitution

'... Federal Employees' Entrance! They Prefer Not To Hobnob With The Riffraff!'

LOU GRANT
Oakland Tribune
©Los Angeles Times Syndicate

CARL LARSEN
Courtesy Richmond Times-Dispatch

HERC FICKLEN
©Avalon Features

JERRY BARNETT
Courtesy Indianapolis News

Medicine

The year 1977 saw a long and heated argument in Congress over government funds for abortions. Finally, on December 7, both houses approved limited payments for abortions in some medical emergencies and for women who are victims of rape or incest.

At least one heartening fact came to light during the year—there is no longer a shortage of doctors nationwide, or of hospital beds. Medical schools have doubled their enrollments since 1960, and the number of practicing physicians has risen 30 percent in the past five years. Medical costs, however, have climbed at a rate 50 percent greater than the cost of living.

Many instances of Medicare and Medicaid abuse surfaced during the year. Investigations indicated that a relatively few doctors, nursing home operators, druggists, and laboratories were defrauding taxpayers of more than $1 billion each year.

Spending for health care increased at a startling rate. While Americans spent $69.2 billion on health care in 1970, that figure had risen to $160 billion by 1977. Americans are getting the best health care ever, but the big problem remains: how can the average person pay for it?

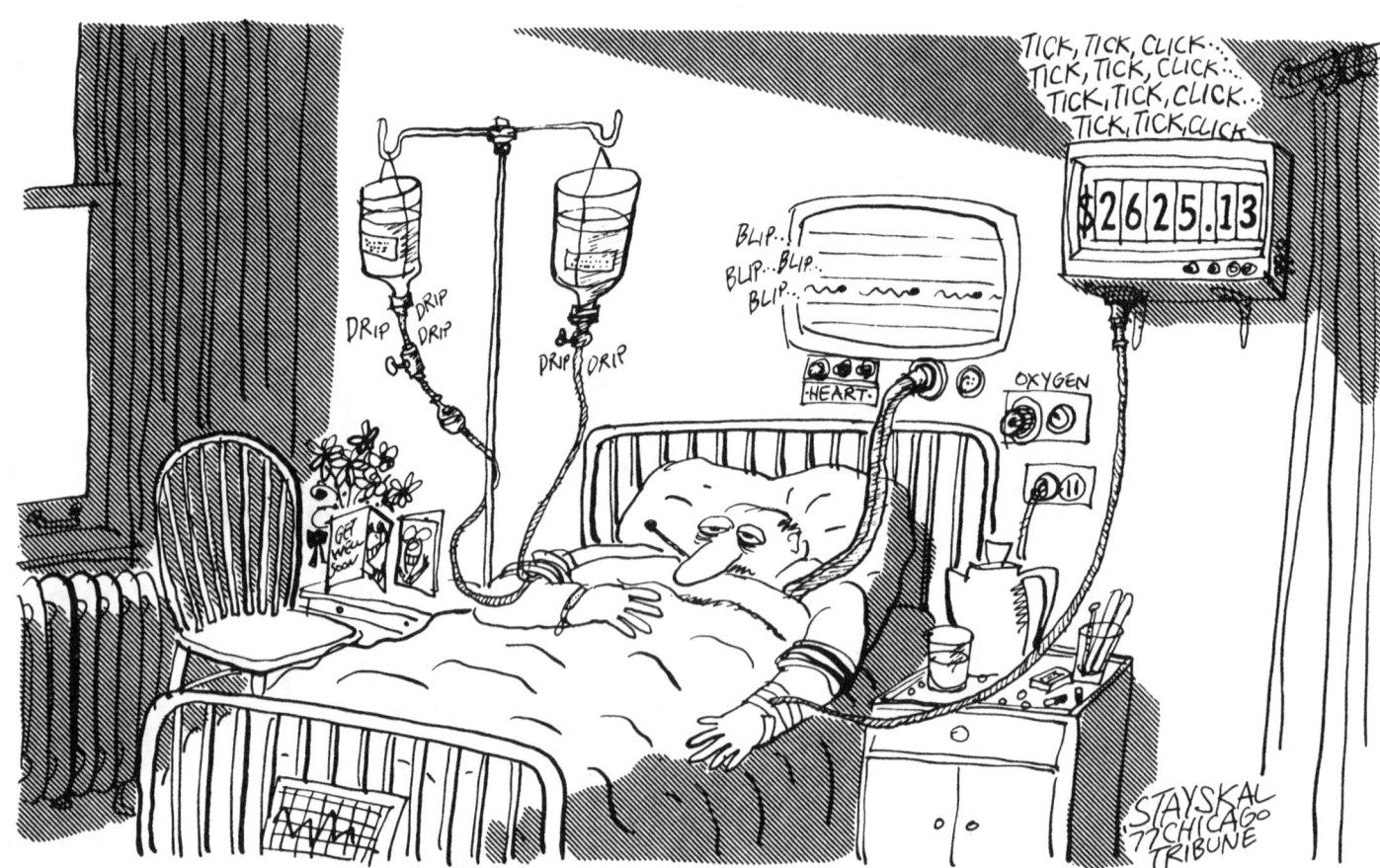

WAYNE STAYSKAL
Courtesy Chicago Tribune

"Oh Boy—Look What's Next on the Menu—National Health Insurance."

ED ASHLEY
Courtesy Toledo Blade

JIM PALMER
Courtesy Dallas News

"When did you begin to think you were eating too many chemicals, additives and grease?"

JIM BERRY
©NEA

CHARLES BISSELL
Courtesy Nashville Tennessean

"You're The Rat That Sickens On Saccharin—I'm The Rat That Flourishes On Laetrile ... Pleased To Meet You!"

JIM PALMER
Courtesy Dallas News

TOM FLANNERY
Courtesy Baltimore Sun

'THE SENATE SENT ME'

CRAIG MACINTOSH
Courtesy Minneapolis Star

Concorde

Transportation Secretary Brock Adams on September 23 announced a plan that allows the controversial supersonic Concorde jet to serve several American cities beginning in early 1978. Previously the Concorde was allowed to land only at Dulles International Airport near Washington, D.C. Tests have shown that the Concorde is twice as noisy on takeoff as other jet aircraft.

Environmentalists denounced this more relaxed policy regarding the Anglo-French plane.

FINALLY AT REST

SUPERSONICATUS TRANSPORTUM
(ORIGIN BRITISH-FRENCH)
...ONCE MASTER OF THE SKIES.
VICTIM OF METAL FATIGUE ACTUATED BY WORLDWIDE SEARCH FOR A PLACE TO LAND.
EXTINCTION INDUCED BY U.S. COURTS AND BUREAUCRATIC BUNGLERS.

JERRY BARNETT
Courtesy Indianapolis News

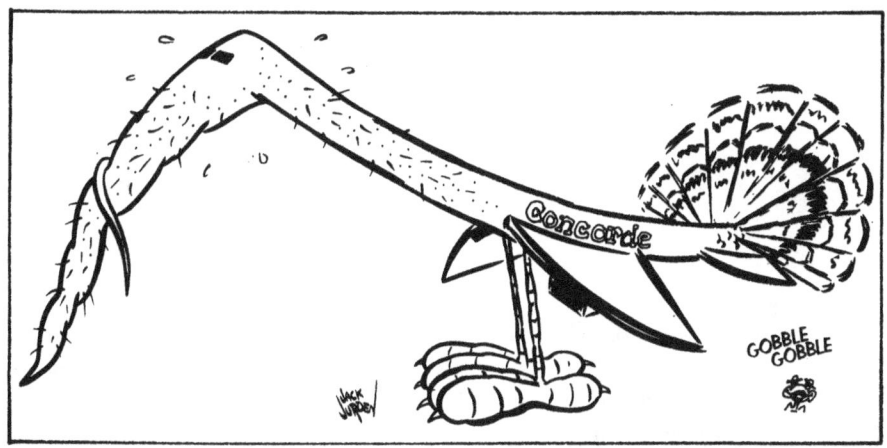

JACK JURDEN
Courtesy Wilmington Evening Journal-News

ED FISCHER
Courtesy Omaha World-Herald

BILL DE ORE
Courtesy Dallas Morning News

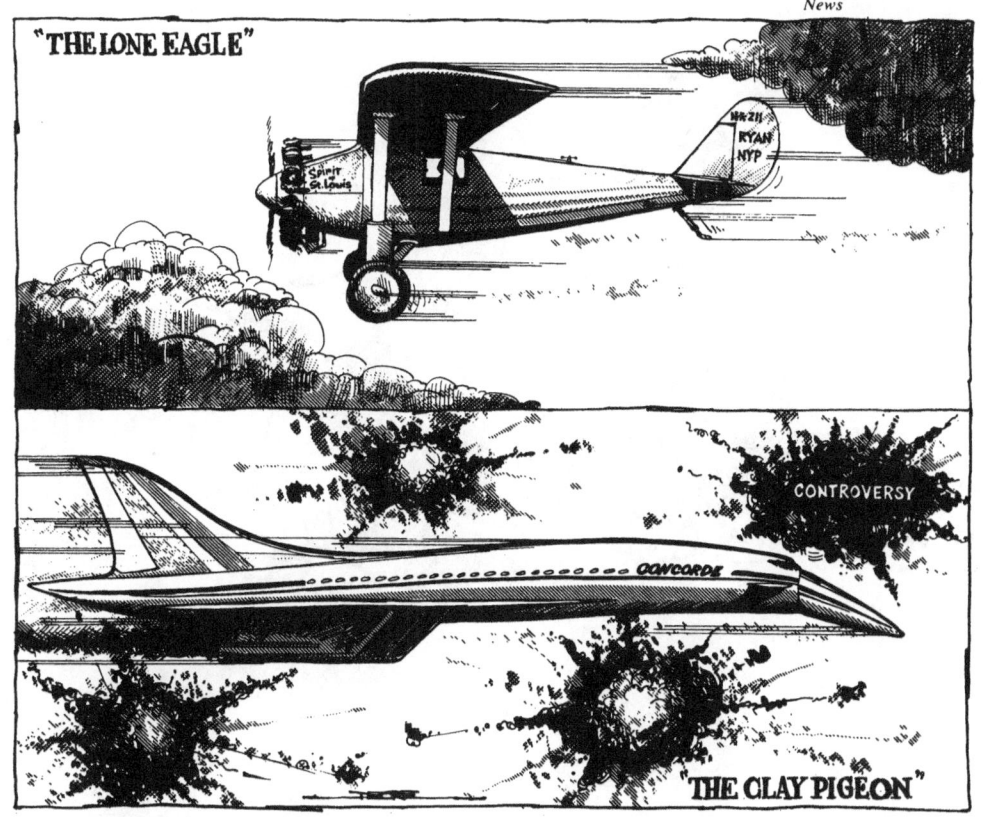

In Memoriam

The year 1977 saw the passing of many well-known personalities, particularly in the world of entertainment. Among them were three of Hollywood's most dazzling stars: Bing Crosby, Charlie Chaplin, and Elvis Presley. Other entertainers who died included Groucho Marx, Alfred Lunt, Joan Crawford, Zero Mostel, Leopold Stokowski, Maria Callas, Guy Lombardo, Andy Devine, Eddie "Rochester" Anderson, Rosalind Russell, and Sebastian Cabot.

Death claimed many other well-known figures, including Anthony Eden, Ludwig Erhard, Louis Untermeyer, P.K. Wrigley, James Jones, and Dr. Wernher von Braun, a major contributor to the U.S. space program.

DWANE POWELL
Courtesy News and Observer

BERT WHITMAN
Courtesy Phoenix Gazette

"White Christmas"

ELDON PLETCHER
New Orleans Times-Picayune
©Rothco

JIM LANGE
The Daily Oklahoman
©The Oklahoma Publishing Co.

LOU GRANT
Oakland Tribune
©Los Angeles Times Syndicate

JOHN RIEDELL
Courtesy Peoria Journal

ROB LAWLOR
Courtesy Philadelphia Daily News

CHARLES BROOKS
Courtesy Birmingham (Ala.) News

... And Other Issues

JEFF MACNELLY
Richmond News Leader
©Chicago Tribune—New York
News Syndicate

JACK JURDEN
Courtesy Wilmington Evening Journal-News

ROBERT GRAYSMITH
Courtesy San Francisco Chronicle

"Tell me again how it was back in 1977 before we ran out of everything"

THE VALLEY OF THE SHADOW

ART WOOD
Courtesy U. S. Independent Telephone Assn.

DOUG SNEYD
Courtesy Toronto Star

"They took everything except the sterling."

HUGH HAYNIE
Louisville Courier-Journal
©Los Angeles Times Syndicate

JOHN MILT MORRIS
©The Associated Press

KATE PALMER
Courtesy Greenville (S.C.) News

LOU ERICKSON
Courtesy Atlanta Journal

'HOW COME YOU AIN'T SCARED OF ME? THIS AIN'T NO DISGUISE . . . IT'S THE REAL THING!'

JACK McLEOD
Courtesy Buffalo Evening News

'THIS WINTER IT SEEMED MORE SENSIBLE THAN BUYING A DOG'

Frosty the Pickpocket

CARL LARSEN
Courtesy Richmond Times-Dispatch

ALBERTO HUICI
Courtesy Jueves de Excelsior (Mex.)

Past Award Winners

PULITZER PRIZE EDITORIAL CARTOON

1922—Rollin Kirby, New York World
1924—J. N. Darling, New York Herald Tribune
1925—Rollin Kirby, New York World
1926—D. R. Fitzpatrick, St. Louis Post-Dispatch
1927—Nelson Harding, Brooklyn Eagle
1928—Nelson Harding, Brooklyn Eagle
1929—Rollin Kirby, New York World
1930—Charles Macauley, Brooklyn Eagle
1931—Edmund Duffy, Baltimore Sun
1932—John T. McCutcheon, Chicago Tribune
1933—H. M. Talburt, Washington Daily News
1934—Edmund Duffy, Baltimore Sun
1935—Ross A. Lewis, Milwaukee Journal
1937—C. D. Batchelor, New York Daily News
1938—Vaughn Shoemaker, Chicago Daily News
1939—Charles G. Werner, Daily Oklahoman
1940—Edmund Duffy, Baltimore Sun
1941—Jacob Burck, Chicago Times
1942—Herbert L. Block, Newspaper Enterprise Association
1943—Jay N. Darling, New York Herald Tribune
1944—Clifford K. Berryman, Washington Star
1945—Bill Mauldin, United Feature Syndicate
1946—Bruce Russell, Los Angeles Times
1947—Vaughn Shoemaker, Chicago Daily News
1948—Reuben L. (Rube) Goldberg, New York Sun
1949—Lute Pease, Newark Evening News
1950—James T. Berryman, Washington Star
1951—Reginald W. Manning, Arizona Republic
1952—Fred L. Packer, New York Mirror
1953—Edward D. Kuekes, Cleveland Plain Dealer
1954—Herbert L. Block, Washington Post
1955—Daniel R. Fitzpatrick, St. Louis Post-Dispatch
1956—Robert York, Louisville Times
1957—Tom Little, Nashville Tennessean
1958—Bruce M. Shanks, Buffalo Evening News
1959—Bill Mauldin, St. Louis Post-Dispatch
1961—Carey Orr, Chicago Tribune
1962—Edmund S. Valtman, Hartford Times
1963—Frank Miller, Des Moines Register
1964—Paul Conrad, Denver Post
1966—Don Wright, Miami News
1967—Patrick B. Oliphant, Denver Post

1968—Eugene Gray Payne, Charlotte Observer
1969—John Fischetti, Chicago Daily News
1970—Thomas F. Darcy, Newsday
1971—Paul Conrad, Los Angeles Times
1972—Jeffrey K. MacNelly, Richmond News Leader
1974—Paul Szep, Boston Globe
1975—Garry Trudeau, Universal Press Syndicate
1976—Tony Auth, Philadelphia Enquirer
1977—Paul Szep, Boston Globe

NOTE: Pulitzer Prize Award was not given 1923, 1936, 1960, 1965, and 1973.

SIGMA DELTA CHI AWARDS EDITORIAL CARTOON

1942—Jacob Burck, Chicago Times
1943—Charles Werner, Chicago Sun
1944—Henry Barrow, Associated Press
1945—Reuben L. Goldberg, New York Sun
1946—Dorman H. Smith, Newspaper Enterprise Association
1947—Bruce Russell, Los Angeles Times
1948—Herbert Block, Washington Post
1949—Herbert Block, Washington Post
1950—Bruce Russell, Los Angeles Times
1951—Herbert Block, Washington Post, and Bruce Russell, Los Angeles Times
1952—Cecil Jensen, Chicago Daily News
1953—John Fischetti, Newspaper Enterprise Association
1954—Calvin Alley, Memphis Commercial Appeal
1955—John Fischetti, Newspaper Enterprise Association
1956—Herbert Block, Washington Post
1957—Scott Long, Minneapolis Tribune
1958—Clifford H. Baldowski, Atlanta Constitution
1959—Charles G. Brooks, Birmingham News
1960—Dan Dowling, New York Herald-Tribune
1961—Frank Interlandi, Des Moines Register
1962—Paul Conrad, Denver Post
1963—William Mauldin, Chicago Sun-Times
1964—Charles Bissell, Nashville Tennessean
1965—Roy Justus, Minneapolis Star
1966—Patrick Oliphant, Denver Post
1967—Eugene Payne, Charlotte Observer

1968—Paul Conrad, Los Angeles Times
1969—William Mauldin, Chicago Sun-Times
1970—Paul Conrad, Los Angeles Times
1971—Hugh Haynie, Louisville Courier-Journal
1972—William Mauldin, Chicago Sun-Times
1973—Paul Szep, Boston Globe
1974—Mike Peters, Dayton Daily News
1975—Tony Auth, Philadelphia Enquirer
1976—Paul Szep, Boston Globe

NATIONAL HEADLINERS CLUB AWARDS EDITORIAL CARTOON

1938—C. D. Batchelor, New York Daily News
1939—John Knott, Dallas News
1940—Herbert Block, Newspaper Enterprise Association
1941—Charles H. Sykes, Philadelphia Evening Ledger
1942—Jerry Doyle, Philadelphia Record
1943—Vaughn Shoemaker, Chicago Daily News
1944—Roy Justus, Sioux City Journal
1945—F. O. Alexander, Philadelphia Bulletin
1946—Hank Barrow, Associated Press
1947—Cy Hungerford, Pittsburgh Post-Gazette
1948—Tom Little, Nashville Tennessean
1949—Bruce Russell, Los Angeles Times
1950—Dorman Smith, Newspaper Enterprise Association
1951—C. G. Werner, Indianapolis Star
1952—John Fischetti, Newspaper Enterprise Association
1953—James T. Berryman and Gib Crockett, Washington Star
1954—Scott Long, Minneapolis Tribune
1955—Leo Thiele, Los Angeles Mirror-News
1956—John Milt Morris, Associated Press
1957—Frank Miller, Des Moines Register
1958—Burris Jenkins, Jr., New York Journal-American
1959—Karl Hubenthal, Los Angeles Examiner
1960—Don Hesse, St. Louis Globe-Democrat
1961—L. D. Warren, Cincinnati Enquirer
1962—Franklin Morse, Los Angeles Mirror
1963—Charles Bissell, Nashville Tennessean
1964—Lou Grant, Oakland Tribune
1965—Merle R. Tingley, London (Ont.) Free Press
1966—Hugh Haynie, Louisville Courier-Journal
1967—Jim Berry, Newspaper Enterprise Association
1968—Warren King, New York News
1969—Larry Barton, Toledo Blade
1970—Bill Crawford, Newspaper Enterprise Association
1971—Ray Osrin, Cleveland Plain Dealer
1972—Jacob Burck, Chicago Sun-Times
1973—Ranan Lurie, New York Times
1974—Tom Darcy, Newsday
1975—Bill Sanders, Milwaukee Journal
1976—No award given
1977—Paul Szep, Boston Globe

NATIONAL NEWSPAPER AWARD/CANADA

1949—Jack Boothe, Toronto Globe and Mail
1950—James G. Reidford, Montreal Star
1951—Len Norris, Vancouver Sun
1952—Robert La Palme, Le Devoir, Montreal
1953—Robert W. Chambers, Halifax Chronicle-Herald
1954—John Collins, Montreal Gazette
1955—Merle R. Tingley, London Free Press
1956—James G. Reidford, Toronto Globe and Mail
1957—James G. Reidford, Toronto Globe and Mail
1958—Raoul Hunter, Le Soleil, Quebec
1959—Duncan Macpherson, Toronto Star
1960—Duncan Macpherson, Toronto Star
1961—Ed McNally, Montreal Star
1962—Duncan Macpherson, Toronto Star
1963—Jan Kamienski, Winnipeg Tribune
1964—Ed McNally, Montreal Star
1965—Duncan Macpherson, Toronto Star
1966—Robert W. Chambers, Halifax Chronicle-Herald
1967—Raoul Hunter, Le Soleil, Quebec
1968—Roy Peterson, Vancouver Sun
1969—Edward Uluschak, Edmonton Journal
1970—Duncan Macpherson, Toronto Daily Star
1971—Yardley Jones, Toronto Sun
1972—Duncan Macpherson, Toronto Star
1973—John Collins, Montreal Gazette
1974—Blaine, Hamilton Spectator
1975—Roy Peterson, Vancouver Sun
1976—Andy Donato, Toronto Sun

Index

Aguila, Dani, 88
Alexander, Ken, 89, 91, 120, 137
Andrews, Bill, 76, 109, 110
Artley, Bob, 32, 72
Ashley, Ed, 121, 143

Baldy (Baldowski), 67, 71, 124, 140
Barnett, Jerry, 141, 146
Basset, Gene, 39, 66, 94, 119
Beckett, Bob, 94, 132
Bender, Jack, 46, 49, 65
Berry, Jim, 19, 44, 99, 143
Bimrose, Art, 42, 68
Bissell, Charles, 67, 126, 144
Bittle, Jerry, 57, 75
Blaine, 96, 116, 127, 137
Borgman, Jim, 29, 36, 90
Borozwski, Len, 34, 115
Brodner, Steve, 100
Brooks, Charles, 48, 53, 62, 150

Campbell, Sandy, 79, 100
Cantone, Vic, 135, 136
Collins, John, 126, 127
Commodore, Chester, 132, 136
Craig, Eugene, 42, 140
Crawford, John, 101, 107, 136
Cunnington, Merle, 16, 99
Curtis, Tom, 14, 23, 50, 83

Daniel, Charles, 28, 99
Day, Bill, 50, 135
Dean, Pap, 83
De Ore, Bill, 20, 33, 147
Dobbins, Jim, 64, 106, 110
Donato, Andy, 10, 14, 30, 126
Doyle, Jerry, 101
Drebelbis, Robert, 136

Englehart, Bob, 22, 72, 95, 118
Engelhardt, Tom, 29, 41, 61, 94
Erickson, Lou, 108, 155

Fearing, Jerry, 101, 104
Ficklen, Herc, 40, 141
Fischer, Ed, 41, 53, 98, 147
Fischetti, John, 31, 51, 105, 118, back cover
Fisher, George, 47, 57
Flannery, Tom, 50, 143, 145

Gamble, Ed, 21, 65, 108, 131
Garner, Bill, 43, 77, 98, 116
Germano, Eddie, 79
Graham, Bill, 19, 40, 110
Grant, Lou, 115, 137, 141, 150
Graysmith, Robert, 121, 153, front cover

Harrington, Ollie, 44, 47, 107
Harsh, Lew, 85, 110, 121
Haynie, Hugh, 15, 78, 91, 154
Henrikson, Art, 41, 58
Hesse, Don, 21, 44, 50, 59
Hill, Draper, 57, 66, 80, 115
Hubenthal, Karl, 17, 35, 74, 139
Huici, Alberto, 58, 156
Hulme, Etta, 29, 65, 109
Humphrey, Bryon, 74, 122
Hungerford, Cy, 6

Interlandi, Frank, 46, 49, 58, 88
Ivy, Jim, 19, 52

Jenkins, Anthony, 63, 114
Judge, Lee, 69, 92, 135
Jurden, Jack, 147, 153

INDEX

Keefe, Mike, 28, 38, 91, 138
Kennedy, Jon, 124, 134, 138
Knudsen, Jim, 60, 69

Lane, John, 28, 68, 129
Lange, Jim, 24, 149
Larsen, Chick, 35, 141, 156
Lawlor, Rob, 32, 112, 128, 150
LePelley, Gurnsey, 67, 75, 83, 85
Liederman, Al, 55
Locher, Dick, 51, 54, 103, 117
Long, Scott, 49, 54, 96
Lynch, Dan, 18, 31

MacIntosh, Craig, 35, 129, 145
MacNelly, Jeff, 13, 73, 97, 152
McLeod, Jack, 15, 63, 156
McVey, Kevin, 58
Manning, Reg, 36, 70, 133
Maples, Harold, 81, 122
Margulies, Jimmy, 92
Menees, Tim, 32, 60, 62
Morgan, Jim, 92
Morin, Jim, 42, 56
Morris, John Milt, 22, 100, 155

Nobile, Ricky, 36
Norris, Leonard, 103, 130

Orton, Jim, 138
Osrin, Ray, 26, 52, 75, 95

Palmer, Jim, 102, 143, 144
Palmer, Kate, 33, 68, 155
Peterson, Clyde, 53, 55, 111, 116
Peterson, Roy, 30, 127
Pletcher, Eldon, 81, 149
Poinier, Art, 104, 113, 129
Powell, Dwane, 77, 89, 148

Rawls, S. C., 23, 27, 85, 97
Renault, Dennis, 44, 61, 129
Riedell, John, 20, 150
Robinson, Jerry, 37, 72
Roschkov, V., 73, 84, 126
Rosen, Hy, 26, 82, 113
Runtz, Vic, 86, 130

Sargent, Ben, 53, 55, 140
Seavey, David, 45, 69, 81
Shevchik, John, 40
Smith, Eric, 40
Sneyd, Doug, 52, 60, 154
Solano, William, 67
Spangler, Frank, 76, 124
Stampone, John, 82, 108
Stayskal, Wayne, 20, 37, 132, 142
Sullivan, Bob, 24, 63, 133
Szep, Paul, 8, 9, 27, 106

Taylor, Bob, 25, 79, 119
Thompson, Vern, 22, 70, 87, 113
Tingley, Merle, 88, 107
Trever, John, 76, 117

Uluschak, Edd, 52, 87, 125

Valtman, Ed, 18, 61, 151

Wallmeyer, Dick, 82, 86, 102
Wells, Clyde, 30, 123
Werner, Charles, 16, 32, 88, 104
Westphal, Ken, 63, 86
Whitman, Bert, 16, 112, 149
Wicks, Ben, 16, 46
Williams, Frank, 68, 102
Wood, Art, 21, 23, 154
Wright, Dick, 39, 45, 74, 80
Wright, Larry, 47, 106, 124